I Care for My Community

Katie Peters

GRL Consultants,
Diane Craig and Monica Marx,
Certified Literacy Specialists

Lerner Publications ◆ Minneapolis

Note from a GRL Consultant

This Pull Ahead leveled book has been carefully designed for beginning readers. A team of guided reading literacy experts has reviewed and leveled the book to ensure readers pull ahead and experience success.

Lerner Publications
An imprint of Lerner Publishing Group, Inc.
241 First Avenue North
Minneapolis, MN 55401 USA

For reading levels and more information, look up this title at www.lernerbooks.com.

Main body text set in Memphis Pro 24/39
Typeface provided by Linotype.

Photo Acknowledgments
The images in this book are used with the permission of: © bojanstory/Getty Images, pp. 4–5, 16 (center); © LPETTET/Getty Images, pp. 8–9; © Makidotvn/Getty Images, pp. 12–13, 16 (right); © Pixel-Shot/Shutterstock Images, p. 3; © Ridofranz/Getty Images, pp. 10–11; © Viorel Kurnosov/Getty Images, pp. 6–7, 16 (left); © Wavebreakmedia/Getty Images, pp. 14–15.

Front cover: Rawpixel.com/Shutterstock Images.

Library of Congress Cataloging-in-Publication Data

Names: Peters, Katie, author.
Title: I care for my community / Katie Peters.
Description: Minneapolis, MN : Lerner Publications, [2023] | Series: I care (Pull Ahead Readers People Smarts—nonfiction) | Includes index. | Audience: Ages 4–7 | Audience: Grades K–1 | Summary: "People in a community help each other out. Early readers can explore ways to care for their community in this easily accessible text. Pairs with the fiction book, Our Garden"— Provided by publisher.
Identifiers: LCCN 2021044321 (print) | LCCN 2021044322 (ebook) | ISBN 9781728457666 (library binding) | ISBN 9781728461502 (ebook)
Subjects: LCSH: Community life—Juvenile literature. | Community development—Juvenile literature. | Caring—Juvenile literature.
Classification: LCC HM761 .P466 2023 (print) | LCC HM761 (ebook) | DDC 307—dc23

LC record available at https://lccn.loc.gov/2021044321
LC ebook record available at https://lccn.loc.gov/2021044322

Manufactured in the United States of America
1 – CG – 7/15/22

Table of Contents

I Care for My Community

This dress is too small.
I give it away so another
kid can wear it.

I don't read this book anymore. I give it to a friend to read.

Firefighters help keep our community safe. I send them thank-you cards.

My grandpa is sick. I draw pictures to cheer him up.

My neighbor needs
help around her house.
I water her flowers.

There are many ways I can care for my community.

How do you help the people in your community?

Did You See It?

book

dress

flowers

Index